THE LIZARD LIBRARY™

The Leopard Gecko

Jake Miller

The Rosen Publishing Group's

PowerKids Press™

New York

Published in 2003 by The Rosen Publishing Group, Inc.
29 East 21st Street, New York, NY 10010

First Edition

Project Editor: Nancy MacDonell Smith
Book Design: Maria E. Melendez

Photo Credits: Cover and title page, p. 22, © Joe McDonald/CORBIS; p. 4 © Gallo Images/CORBIS; pp. 5, 10, 14, 20 (bottom) © David A. Northcott/CORBIS; p. 11 © Papilio/CORBIS; p. 6 © Martin Harvey/Peter Arnold, Inc.; pp. 7, 8, 9, 12, 15 (bottom); pp. 13, 15 (top) James Gerholdt/Peter Arnold, Inc.; p. 16 © R. Andrew Odum/Peter Arnold, Inc.; 19 © Zig Leszczynsky/Animals, Animals; p. 20 (top) © Digital Stock; borders © Digital Vision.

Miller, Jake, 1969–
The leopard gecko / Jake Miller.— 1st ed.
    p. cm. — (The Lizard library)
Includes bibliographical references (p.   ).
Summary: Describes the life cycle and habits of the leopard gecko.
  ISBN 0-8239-6413-2 (lib. bdg.)
1. Leopard gecko—Juvenile literature. [1. Leopard gecko.] I. Title.
  QL666.L245 M55 2003
  597.95'2—dc21
                                                              2001007782

Manufactured in the United States of America

Contents

1   That Lizard Looks Like a Leopard!   5

2   A Different Kind of Gecko   6

3   Down to Earth   9

4   Night Lizards   10

5   Baby Geckos   13

6   The Cycle of Life   14

7   Living Together   17

8   Hunters in the Dark   18

9   Hunting the Hunter   21

10   Leopard Geckos Make Great Pets   22

    Glossary   23

    Index   24

    Web Sites   24

Above: Along with their triangle-shaped heads, leopard geckos have stocky bodies and fat tails. Right: Most leopard geckos weigh less than 2 ounces (57 g).

That Lizard Looks Like a Leopard!

It's easy to see where leopard geckos get their name. Their bodies have dark brown or black spots on a yellow background, as does a leopard's. Leopard geckos are members of the gecko family of lizards. Most lizards have pointy, narrow heads that look like they grow right out of their bodies. Leopard geckos have triangular heads and necks. They have four thin legs, and five thin toes on each foot. Their toes have claws. The biggest leopard geckos grow to be about 12 inches (30 cm) long, but most are between 7 inches and 10 inches (18 cm–25 cm) long. Their skin is dry and soft.

A Different Kind of Gecko

There are 700 **species** of geckos in the world. The scientific name for leopard geckos is *Eublepharis macularius*. The leopard gecko's species name, *macularius*, means "spotted." Their **genus** is *Eublepharis*. *Eublepharis* is Latin for "true eyelid." One thing that makes leopard geckos different from other geckos is that leopard geckos have real eyelids. Some geckos don't have eyelids at all. Others have a clear eyelid that is always shut. Leopard gecko eyelids are not clear, so they can't see through them. They close their eyes to go to sleep. One other difference is that most geckos have sticky pads on their feet. Leopard geckos have claws on their feet.

Leopard geckos have eyelids that can blink open and shut.

Leopard geckos don't have sticky pads on their feet, so they can't climb walls like other geckos. Instead, they have claws.

This leopard gecko makes its home in the rocky desert of Afghanistan.

Down to Earth

Leopard geckos live in open areas. They like rocks, soil, and grass. Leopard geckos like to live on the ground. They don't climb trees very often. Leopard geckos live in the wild, dry, rocky parts of Iran and Afghanistan in the Middle East. They also live in India and Pakistan in South Asia. The areas where they live are very hard places in which to **survive**. Sometimes there is not enough food to eat. Water is not easy to find. If a leopard gecko finds a lot to eat, it can store extra fat in its tail to use later when food is scarce. Their tails get very big. The fat-tailed gecko is very similar to the leopard gecko. The scientific name for the fat-tailed gecko is *Eublepharis angramainyu*.

Fat-tailed geckos, such as this one, are found in India and in Pakistan.

Night Lizards

Most lizards are active during the day. Most geckos, including leopard geckos, are active at night. Leopard geckos are **nocturnal**. During the day, they hide under rocks or dig holes in the sand to hide from the sun. They also hide from all of the **predators** who are active during the daytime, such as hawks and other birds. Leopard geckos can see clearly even when it's dark. They have some of the best eyesight of any lizard species. Their large eyes take in a lot of light, even when it is very dark. Many lizards can

Leopard geckos have very good eyesight. This means they can hunt at night.

barely see at all, but leopard geckos have better eyesight than people have. They can see as well as cats can. When the sun sets, leopard geckos leave their hiding places. They hunt crickets and other insects that come out at night.

Crickets make a tasty meal for a leopard gecko.

When the temperature is cooler, about 82°F (28°C), most baby lizards will be female. When it's warmer, 92°F (33°C), most will be males.

Baby Geckos

Baby leopard geckos **hatch** from eggs. When it is time to start a new family, a male leopard gecko looks for a female who is ready to lay her eggs. When he finds her, the male **fertilizes** the female's eggs. Then she begins to lay the eggs. She lays one or two eggs at a time. She buries the eggs under a pile of sand. She may lay a pair of eggs every month for four or five months. The eggs aren't hard like chicken eggs. They are soft like stale marshmallows. The eggshell feels like paper or thin leather.

Whether an egg will contain a male gecko or a female gecko depends on the **temperature** of the air. The difference in temperature changes the way the baby lizards grow inside the eggs.

Baby leopard geckos are only about 3 ½ inches (9 cm) long when they're born.

13

The Cycle of Life

As do most lizards, a **hatchling** gecko knows how to hunt and how to take care of itself as soon as it hatches. When a leopard gecko hatches, it looks quite different from an adult leopard gecko. Instead of spots, the youngsters have stripes. The lizards look more like tigers than they do like leopards. As leopard geckos grow, the stripes fade and are replaced by spots. Leopard geckos grow to full size in about 18 months. They can start having babies of their own before they are even a year old. Most leopard geckos, though, don't have babies until they are a little older. Leopard geckos can live to be nearly 30 years old.

This hatchling has colorful markings, but they will fade as it gets older.

This hatchling is breaking out of its egg. The eggshell is soft but it's still a struggle for the baby gecko to hatch.

As soon as the baby leopard gecko has broken free of the eggshell, it goes off in search of food. Leopard geckos can look after themselves as soon as they're born.

This leopard gecko lives in Asia.

Living Together

Some leopard geckos live alone, but most often they live together in loose groups. A single male will share his space with many females, but males cannot stand to live together. If two males see each other, they will bob their heads up and down. This is a warning sign. If neither of the males backs down after the head bobbing, they will fight. Females will not fight over space, but they will protect their eggs by fighting other lizards. Young leopard geckos act in a certain way when they are angry or scared. They make a hissing noise, raise their tails, and stand with their legs straight out. They open their mouths wide and try to look as big and scary as they can. Older geckos are more likely to make noises to scare away attackers. Geckos almost never attack humans, but when they are angry they sometimes bite.

Hunters in the Dark

Leopard geckos are well **adapted** to hunting in the dark. They can see well in very little light. When they are hunting, leopard geckos act just like cats, another kind of predator that hunts at night. Leopard geckos **stalk** their **prey** quietly. In the dark, the animal that the gecko is hunting can't tell that the silent gecko is nearby. When they are ready to strike, leopard geckos wiggle their tails the way cats do, and then they **pounce**. They survive by hunting insects, but they will eat any small animal they can catch. They eat spiders, other lizards, birds, bird eggs, and even scorpions. Sometimes they eat fruit. Most leopard geckos eat only the insects that they got used to eating when they were babies, though. They have trouble adapting to changes in their diets.

As you can see from its markings, this leopard gecko is not quite full grown.

Leopard Geckos Make Great Pets

Leopard geckos are one of the most popular lizards to keep as pets. They are small. They are easy to care for. They are gentle, and they rarely bite. Lizards are not as cuddly and friendly as cats and dogs, but leopard geckos are friendly lizards. Many kinds of lizards will never become friendly to their owners. Leopard geckos will recognize their owners when they come into a room. These geckos are also fun to watch. They love to explore their homes. They are exciting hunters. They sneak up on a cricket and pounce, just the way a real leopard would pounce on its prey.

Pet leopard geckos will sometimes sit on their owners' shoulders.

22

Glossary

adapted (uh-DAPT-id) Changed to fit new conditions.

Eublepharis angramainyu (YU-bluh-fair-us an-GRAH-mayn-u) Scientific name for the fat-tailed gecko species.

Eublepharis macularius (YU-bluh-fair-us MAK-yu-lar-ee-us) Scientific name for the leopard gecko species.

fertilizes (FUR-tih-ly-ziz) Introduces male reproductive cells into the female to begin development.

genus (JEE-nuhs) The scientific name for a group of similar animals or plants.

habitat (HA-bih-tat) The surroundings where an animal or a plant lives.

hatch (HACH) To come out of an egg.

hatchling (HACH-ling) A young animal that has just come out of the egg.

muscles (MUH-sulz) Parts of the body underneath the skin that can be tightened or loosened to make the body move.

nocturnal (nok-TUR-nul) To be active at night.

pounce (POWNS) To sneak up and jump on something by surprise.

predators (PREH-duh-terz) Animals that kill other animals for food.

prey (PRAY) An animal that is hunted by another animal for food.

species (SPEE-sheez) A single kind of plant or animal. For example, all people are one species.

stalk (STAWK) To find, follow, and sneak up on something.

survive (sur-VYV) To stay alive.

temperature (TEM-pruh-chur) How hot or cold something is.

twitches (TWIH-chiz) Moves suddenly and quickly.

Index

C
claws, 5–6
cricket(s), 11, 22

E
eggs, 13, 17–18
eyelids, 6
eyesight, 11

F
fat-tailed gecko, 9

H
habitat, 21
hatchling, 14
hissing, 17

M
Middle East, 9

N
nocturnal, 10

P
pets, 22
predators, 10, 21
prey, 18, 22

S
South Asia, 9
species, 6

T
tail(s), 9, 17, 21
temperature, 13

Web Sites

Due to the changing nature of Internet links, PowerKids Press has developed an online list of Web sites related to the subject of this book. This site is updated regularly. Please use this link to access the site: www.powerkidspresslinks.com/ll/leopgeck/

To R and F

Copyright © 2018 by Kerascoët

All rights reserved. Published in the United States by Schwartz & Wade Books, an imprint of Random House Children's Books, a division of Penguin Random House LLC, New York.

Schwartz & Wade Books and the colophon are trademarks of Penguin Random House LLC.

Visit us on the Web! rhcbooks.com

Educators and librarians, for a variety of teaching tools, visit us at RHTeachersLibrarians.com

Library of Congress Cataloging-in-Publication Data
Names: Kerascoët, author, illustrator.
Title: I walk with Vanessa / Kerascoët.
Description: First edition. I New York : Schwartz & Wade Books, 2018. I Summary: An elementary school girl witnesses the bullying of another girl, but she is not sure how to help.
Identifiers: LCCN 2017010331 (print) I LCCN 2017033163 (ebook) I ISBN 978-1-5247-6957-4 (e-book) I ISBN 978-1-5247-6955-0 (hardback)
ISBN 978-1-5247-6956-7 (hardcover library binding)
Subjects: I CYAC: Stories without words. I Bullying–Fiction. I Schools–Fiction. I Friendship–Fiction. I Kindness–Fiction. I BISAC: JUVENILE FICTION / Social Issues / Bullying. I JUVENILE FICTION / Social Issues / Prejudice & Racism. I JUVENILE FICTION / Social Issues / Friendship.
Classification: LCC PZ7.1.K5093 (ebook) I LCC PZ7.1.K5093 Iaw 2018 (print) I DDC [E]–dc23

The illustrations were rendered in ink and watercolor.

MANUFACTURED IN CHINA
8 10 9 7
First Edition

The authors would like to thank Beth Yohe, Jinnie Spiegler, and the Anti-Defamation League for their help with the anti-bullying information on the last page.

I WALK WITH
VANESSA

A STORY ABOUT A SIMPLE ACT OF KINDNESS

by Kerascoët

schwartz & wade books · new york

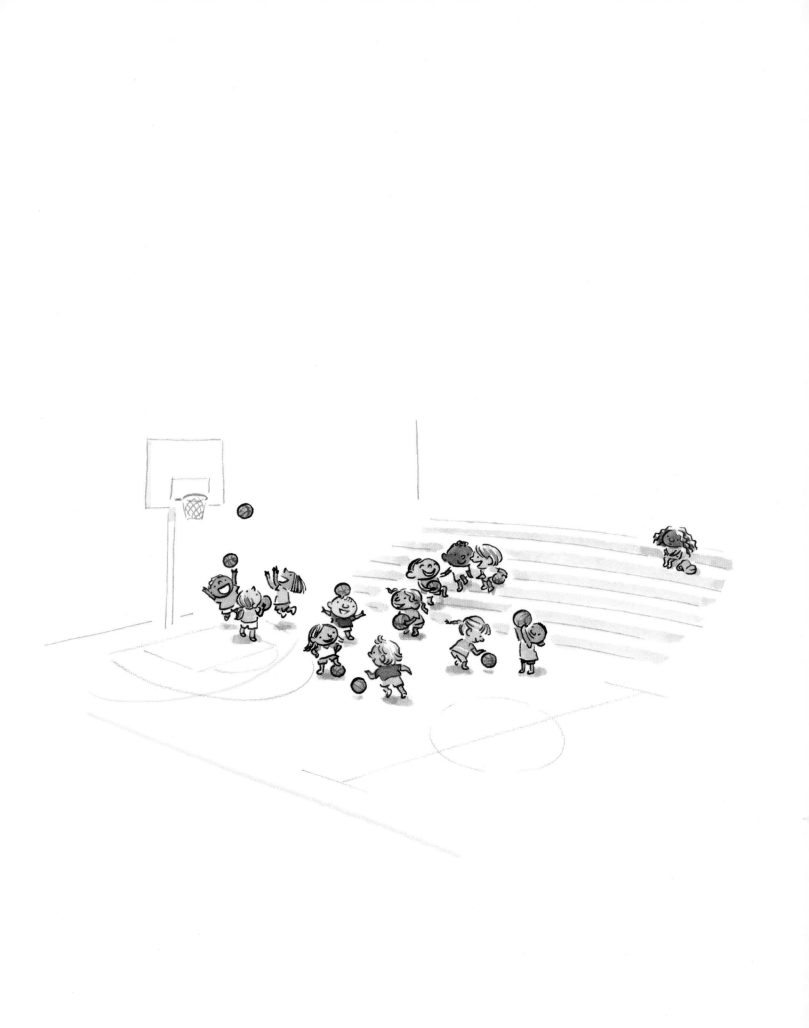

FOR CHILDREN: HOW YOU CAN HELP SOMEONE WHO IS BEING BULLIED

When you see someone being hurt or bullied, there is often something you can do. No matter how small it may seem to you, it makes a big difference to the person who is being hurt. Here are some suggestions:

• Be extra friendly to that person. Include them in your play and games. Let them know you will not join in when other kids are being mean or bullying.

• The girl in this book noticed what happened to the girl who was being bullied. Then she thought about how she might feel and what she should do. When you see mean behavior or bullying, ask yourself, "How would I feel if that happened to me?"

• It is important to always be safe when you respond to bullying behavior. If someone is being hurt or bullied, you can tell a trusted grown-up. Letting someone know help is needed is not tattling. Tattling is getting someone in trouble, and telling is getting someone out of trouble.

• As in the story, actions can be contagious. Kindness multiplies. One small act of kindness can inspire more kind acts, so talk to others about your ideas for showing kindness and invite them to join you.

FOR ADULTS: SOME HELPFUL WORDS TO USE WHEN TALKING ABOUT THIS BOOK WITH CHILDREN

aggressor: Someone who says or does hurtful things.

ally: Someone who helps or stands up for another who is being bullied or is the target of prejudice.

brave: Describes doing something you would not normally do that may be physically or emotionally difficult.

bullying: When a person or group behaves in ways–on purpose, and over and over–that make someone feel hurt, afraid, or embarrassed.

bystander: Someone who sees bullying or prejudice happening and does not say or do anything to stop it.

name-calling: Using words to hurt or be mean to a person or group.

target: Someone who is bullied or treated in hurtful ways by a person or group on purpose, and over and over.

teasing: Laughing at and putting someone down in a way that is either friendly and playful or mean and unkind.

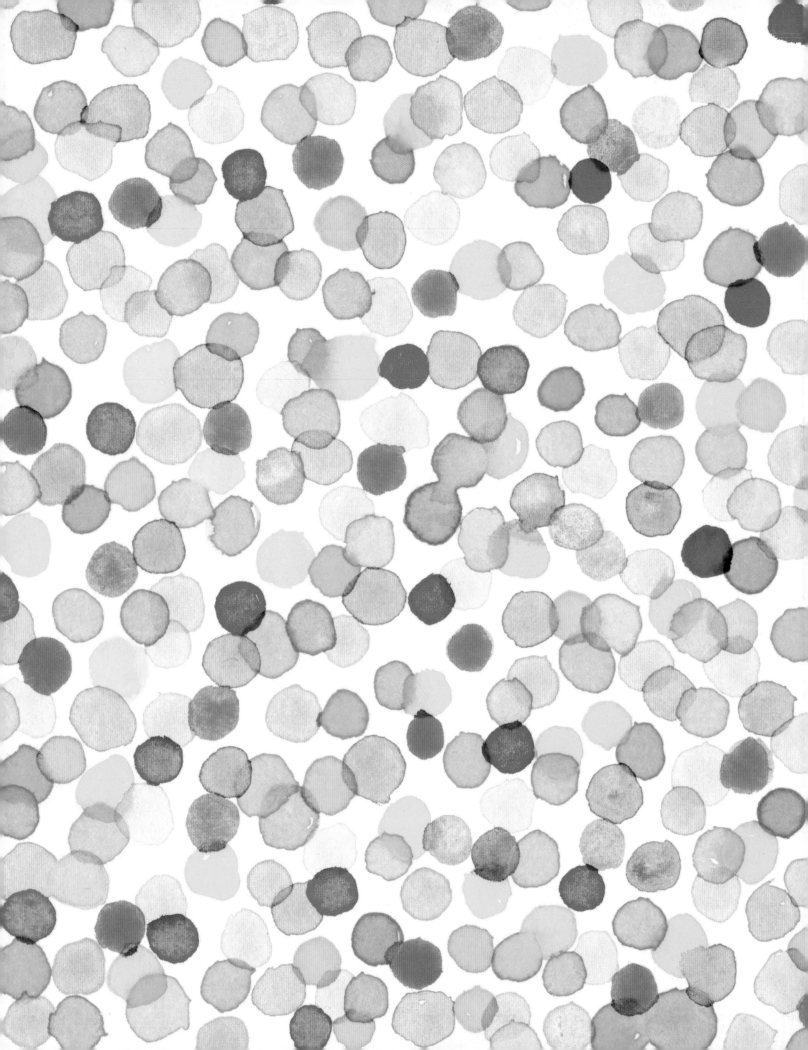